STARS in the SPOTLIGHT

Jake Gyllenhaal

Colleen Adams

PowerKiDS
press™

New York

Published in 2007 by The Rosen Publishing Group, Inc.
29 East 21st Street, New York, NY 10010

Book Design: Haley Wilson

Photo Credits: Cover © Frazer Harrison/Getty Images; pp. 4, 14, 24 © Kevin Winter/Getty Images;
p. 6 © Dan Steinberg/Getty Images; p. 8 © Scott Gries/ImageDirect/Getty Images; p. 10 ©
Newsmakers/Getty Images; p. 12 © Vince Bucci/Getty Images; p. 16 © Peter Kramer/Getty
Images; p. 18 © J. P. Moczulski/AFP/Getty Images; p. 20 © Toru Yamanaka/AFP/Getty Images;
p. 22 © Evan Agostini/Getty Images; p. 26 © Pascal Le Segretain/Getty Images; p. 28 © Steve
Finn/Getty Images.

Library of Congress Cataloging-in-Publication Data

Adams, Colleen.
   Jake Gyllenhaal / Colleen Adams.
      p. cm.
   Includes index.
   ISBN-13: 978-1-4042-3514-0
   ISBN-10: 1-4042-3514-0 (library binding)
   1. Gyllenhaal, Jake, 1980—Juvenile literature. 2. Motion picture actors and actresses–United
States–Biography–Juvenile literature. I. Title.
   PN2287.G95A33 2007
   791.4302'8092-dc22
   [B]
                                    2006014623

Manufactured in the United States of America

Contents

A Talented Actor

Jake Gyllenhaal (JILL-en-hall) established a career in acting at a young age. He is respected by movie **critics** and fans for his talent. Jake is known for his ability to play many different kinds of characters. He got his first acting role when he was in fifth grade. He took other acting roles in movies during his teenage years. Jake's first starring role was in *October Sky* in 1999. His outstanding performances in recent movies such as *Jarhead* and *Brokeback Mountain* have made him well-known. He has received award **nominations** and awards for his work in films.

Jake is shown standing in front of an Oscar statue at the Academy Awards lunch in Beverly Hills, California. He was nominated for an Academy Award for Best Supporting Actor in 2006.

5

Childhood and Family

Jacob Benjamin Gyllenhaal was born on December 19, 1980, in Los Angeles, California. Jake grew up on movie sets because his dad, Stephen Gyllenhaal, is a movie director. His mother, Naomi Foner, is a **screenwriter**. Jake has an older sister named Maggie who is an actress.

Jake and Maggie liked to perform for their friends and family at a young age. Jake grew up having dinner with famous actors and actresses who knew his parents. It was not unusual for him to hang out with actress Jamie Lee Curtis, who is his godmother, or actor Dustin Hoffman. Actor Paul Newman once gave him driving lessons!

Jake is shown with (from left to right) sister Maggie, Mom, and Dad at a dinner in Beverly Hills, California, in 2003.

Early Work as an Actor

Jake made his first appearance in a movie called *City Slickers* in 1991. He played the part of Billy Crystal's son, Danny Robbins. An offer for a part in *Mighty Ducks* came next. However, Jake wasn't in the movie because his parents didn't want him to be away from home for 2 months.

Jake was featured in two of his dad's films. In 1993, he and Maggie played roles in *A Dangerous Woman*. This story was written for the screen by his mom and directed by his dad. Jake appeared in another one of his father's films in 1998.

Jake is shown here at a movie opening with actress Selma Blair.

9

October Sky

In 1999, Jake was chosen for the role of Homer Hickam Jr. in *October Sky*. This true story takes place in the mining town of Coalwood, West Virginia, in 1957. Homer is a gifted high school student who dreams of becoming a rocket scientist. With the help of his friends, Hickam designs and **launches** space rockets. His hard work earns him first prize in a national science fair and money for college. Homer's dad wants him to become a coal miner just like he is. Homer struggles with the decision of whether to follow his dream or win his father's respect. Hickam later became an engineer at NASA and trained astronauts.

In *October Sky*, Jake was in almost every scene. After his performance in this movie, he was no longer an unknown actor.

11

Bubble Boy

Jake graduated from Harvard-Westlake High School in 1998. After the success of *October Sky* in 1999, he received offers for more movies. Jake's parents insisted that he attend college. Jake went to Columbia University in New York City for 2 years. He studied Eastern religions.

Jake continued to take unusual roles in movies that gained him the attention of movie critics and fans. In 2001, Jake was chosen for the role of Jimmy Livingston in an unusual **comedy** called *Bubble Boy*. It is about a boy who lives in a plastic bubble. Jake's decision to play offbeat characters like Jimmy would lead to other roles.

Jake is shown here at the opening of the movie *Bubble Boy* with costar Marley Shelton in 2001.

Taking Chances

Jake made another film in 2001 called *Donnie Darko*. His sister Maggie was also in the film. Jake was nominated for an Independent Spirit Award for Best Actor for his role in this movie. The next year he costarred in a movie with Jennifer Aniston called *The Good Girl*.

His ability to make viewers relate to unusual characters was noticed by directors and fans. Jake wanted to make movies that people would remember because they were different. Jake said, "The truth is, most of the films that make a lot of money no one remembers. I'm not interested in making films that no one remembers."

Jake and costar Jennifer Aniston are shown here at the Hollywood opening of *The Good Girl.*

On Stage!

Jake starred in the play *This Is Our Youth* at the Garrick Theatre in London. Actors Hayden Christensen and Anna Paquin costarred with him. The play ran for 8 weeks. Jake received the 2002 London Evening Standard Theatre Award for Outstanding Newcomer. Jake loves performing on stage. He said, "In the perfect world, I would love to do one play for every three movies." It was Jake's performance in this role that caught the attention of director Sam Mendes. Mendes later cast Jake as Tony Swofford in the movie *Jarhead*.

Jake's performances in movies and on stage showed that he was able to play unusual characters that an audience could relate to.

Moonlight Mile

In 2002, Jake played the part of Joe Nast in *Moonlight Mile*. In the movie, Joe's **fiancée**, Diana, dies suddenly. Joe gets closer to Diana's parents as a way to deal with her death and his feelings. Joe also reveals secrets he has kept from Diana's parents. Jake was praised for his performance. The success of this movie established him as a talented young actor and brought him an offer for a role in *The Day After Tomorrow*.

Jake is shown here in a scene from *Moonlight Mile* with Susan Sarandon and Dustin Hoffman, who played Diana's parents.

The Day After Tomorrow

In 2004, Jake played the role of Sam Hall in *The Day After Tomorrow*. Sam is the son of **climatologist** Jack Hall. Jack researches the effects of **global warming** on Earth. His findings show that sudden and unexpected changes in Earth's climate are about to start a new ice age. When this happens, tornadoes destroy Los Angeles, California, and a huge wave floods New York City. The temperature drops quickly, and everything freezes. Jack races against time to save Sam, who is trapped in New York City. The success of this film brought Jake more offers for challenging roles in 2005.

Jake (far left) costarred in the movie *The Day After Tomorrow* with actor Dennis Quaid and actress Emmy Rossum. They pose for pictures at the movie opening in Japan with director Roland Emmerich (far right).

Proof

Jake made three movies in 2005. *Proof* is the story of Robert and his daughter Catherine. Robert, who is a mathematical **genius**, suffers from a mental illness. Catherine drops out of college to take care of him. When Robert passes away, Catherine must deal with her fear that she may have **inherited** both her father's genius and his mental illness. Jake plays Hal, a former student of Robert's. Hal meets Catherine when he comes to look at some of her father's old notebooks. Hal finds an important **equation** Robert was working on before he died. With Hal's help, Catherine faces her fears and makes important discoveries about herself.

Jake is shown here with Gwyneth Paltrow, who played the part of Catherine in the movie *Proof*, and director John Madden (far right).

Jarhead

Jake went on to star in *Jarhead*, also released in 2005. This movie is based on a best-selling book by Anthony Swofford. In this movie, Jake plays the part of Tony "Swoff" Swofford. As a young marine, Swofford is sent to Saudi Arabia in 1990 to fight in the Gulf War. Swofford must learn about life as a marine. While dealing with the boredom and heat of the desert, Swofford must take orders from Sergeant Sykes. He also makes friends with Corporal Troy, a fellow marine. Jake received great reviews for his performance as Swofford.

Jake is shown here with *Jarhead* director Sam Mendes (middle) and costar Peter Sarsgaard (far right) at a party in Hollywood.

Brokeback Mountain

In *Brokeback Mountain*, Jake plays Jack Twist, a young cowboy who looks for work on a ranch in Wyoming in 1963. He meets Ennis Del Mar, a ranch hand. They are sent to work as sheepherders on Brokeback Mountain. Jack and Ennis develop a close friendship but decide to go their separate ways. Both marry and have families. Ennis and Jack meet again 4 years later. Their relationship lasts for 19 years. Jake received Academy Award and Screen Actors Guild Award nominations for Best Supporting Actor for this role.

Jake is shown here with *Brokeback Mountain* costar Heath Ledger (far left) and director Ang Lee (middle).

The Man Who Walked Between the Towers

Jake's choices of acting projects continue to delight fans everywhere. Jake has taken on some surprising projects that fans may not expect. In 2005, Jake **narrated** an **animated film** for children called *The Man Who Walked Between the Towers*. It is a story about French tightrope walker Phillipe Petit. In 1974, Petit put a tightrope between the World Trade Center's twin towers. He spent an hour entertaining onlookers by walking, dancing, and doing tricks on the high wire.

Jake is shown here signing autographs for fans. Jake's fans are so loyal to him they are often called "Gyllenhaalics."

29

A Bright Future

What's next for Jake? Jake's talent as an actor continues to grow with each role he plays. In 2006, Jake played the role of reporter Robert Graysmith in a movie called *Zodiac*. This movie shows the lives of detectives and newspaper reporters involved in a murder case.

The success of Jake's movie roles in 2005 changed his life as an actor. The praise and honors he has received have made him one of the most respected actors today. Fans can expect more exciting and original performances from Jake in the years to come.

Glossary

animated film (AA-nuh-may-tuhd FILM) A movie made from a series of drawings.

climatologist (kly-muh-TAH-luh-jihst) A scientist who studies the differences and changes in weather patterns.

comedy (KAH-muh-dee) A funny play or movie that has a happy ending.

critic (KRIH-tihk) A person who makes a judgment about the value, worth, beauty, or quality of something.

equation (ih-KWAY-zhun) A statement of the equality of two mathematical expressions.

fiancée (fee-AHN-say) A woman engaged to be married.

genius (JEEN-yuhs) A person who has very high intelligence.

global warming (GLOH-buhl WOHR-ming) An increase in the temperature of Earth's atmosphere and oceans that results from air pollution.

inherit (in-HAIR-uht) To receive features from parents.

launch (LAWNCH) To send off with force.

narrate (NAIR-ayt) To tell a story in full detail.

nomination (nah-muh-NAY-shun) The state of being chosen as a candidate for election, appointment, or honor.

screenwriter (SKREEN-ry-tuhr) Someone who writes movies.

31

Index

Web Sites

Due to the changing nature of Internet links, PowerKids Press has developed
an online list of Web sites related to the subject of this book. This site is
updated regularly. Please use this link to access the list:
http://www.powerkidslinks.com/stars/gyllenhaal/